THE GREAT BIG BOOK OF Pirates

John Malam

QED Publishing

Copyright © QED Publishing 2008
First published in the UK by
QED Publishing
A Quarto Group Company
226 City Road
London EC1V 2TT
www.qed-publishing.co.uk

A catalogue record for this book is available
from the British Library.

ISBN 978 1 84835 121 9

Printed and bound in China

Author John Malam (www.johnmalam.co.uk)
Consultant Philip Steele
Editor Amanda Askew
Designer Lisa Peacock
Picture Researcher Maria Joannou
Illustrators Adam Hook, Richard Hook, Peter Bull,
    Francis Phillips, Mike Saunders

Publisher Steve Evans
Creative Director Zeta Davies

Words in **bold** can be found in
the glossary on page 116.

Picture credits (t=top, b=bottom, r=right, l=left)

Alamy Images Mary Evans Picture Library 10, 11, 22,
Klaus lang 46, Mary Evans Picture Library 54–55, North
Wind Picture Archives 47t, The Print Collector 38r, Mary
Evans Picture Library 69, 76, 84, 86, North Wind Picture
Archives 87, Mary Evans Picture Library 102, 113, 115t,
Visual Arts Library (London) 98

Art Archive Eileen Tweedy 16–17

Bridgeman Art Archive Collection of the
New-York Historical Society 28, Private Collection/
Archives Charmet 20, Private Collection/Peter Newark
Pictures 19, Art Library 48, Private Collection/ Look and
Learn 75, Private Collection, Peter Newark Historical
Pictures 78–79, Yale Center for British Art, Paul Mellon
Collection, USA 81

Corbis Bettmann 29, Charles & Josette
Lenars 27, Historical Picture Archive 30–31, The Gallery
Collection 38l, Bettmann 70, 78, Blue Lantern Studio 68t,
Mansell/Time & Life Pictures 71, 108, Bettmann 98–99,
103, 110, Richard T Nowitz 105t, Tria Giovan 106–107

Getty Images Hulton Archive 24, The Bridgeman Art
Library 14, Hulton Archive 42b, Hulton Archive 97t,
Mansell/Time & Life Pictures 96–97, The Bridgeman Art
Library 107t

Photoshot AISA/World Illustrated 47bl, 47br

Mary Evans Picture Library Grosvenor
Prints 15t

National Maritime Museum 23b

Rex Features Roger-Viollet 18, Sipa Press 115b

Shutterstock 44, 66b, 67b, 68b

Topham Picturepoint The British Museum/HIP 15b,
49t, 53, The Print Collector/HIP 52, 66–67, 83t

CONTENTS

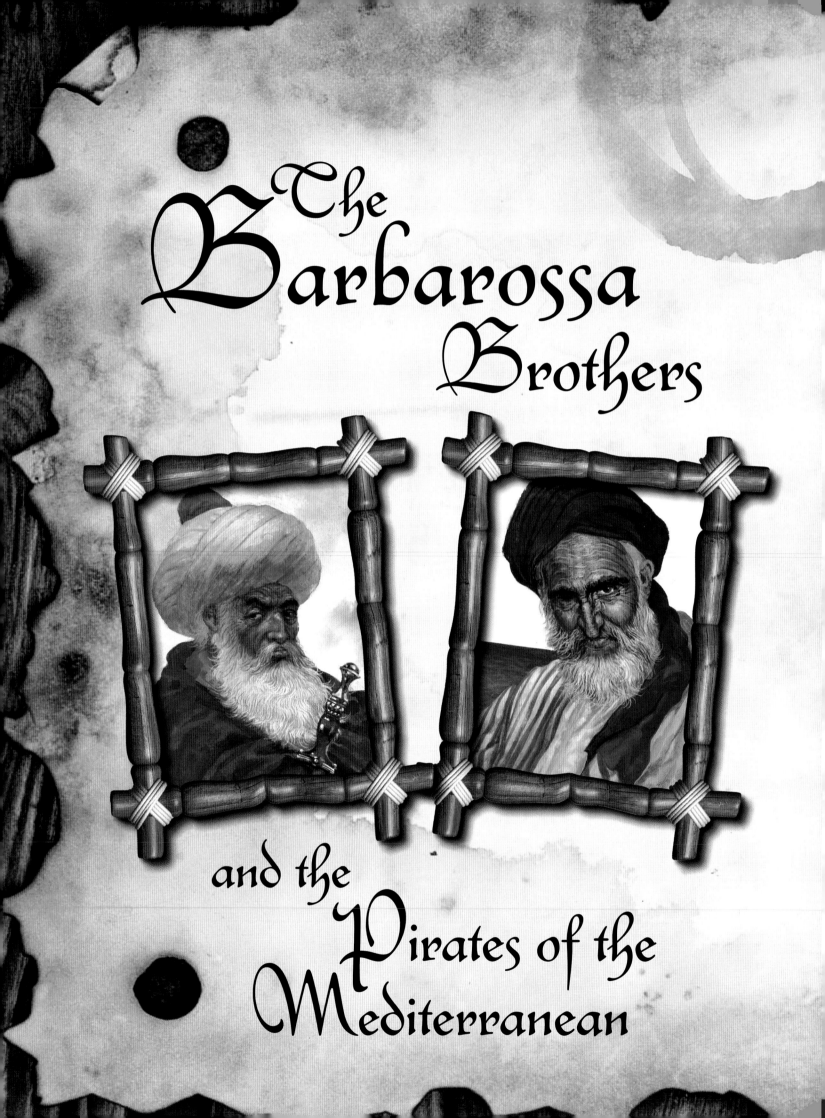

The Barbarossa Brothers

and the Pirates of the Mediterranean

CONTENTS

Pirate attack!

Two large galleys rowed slowly across the water, close to the coast of Italy.

They belonged to Pope Julius II and were carrying his goods. It was a journey that they had made many times before without mishap – but today was to be different.

It was 1504 and as the **papal** ships passed the Italian island of Elba, a small galley began to follow them. At first, the Pope's men on the first ship didn't think much of it, until they saw who was on board. When a look-out spotted that the strangers were wearing **turbans**, panic spread among the **crew**. The small galley was a **Muslim** pirate ship from north Africa, and it preyed on **Christian** ships.

The pirate captain, Aruj **Reis**, brought his galley alongside the larger ship. His men went on board and its crew were taken prisoner. Aruj and his men then disguised themselves in their captives' clothes – it tricked the second galley's crew, and they too were captured.

◄ *The galley of Aruj Reis closes in on the larger galley belonging to Pope Julius II. It was a daring attack.*

Aruj Reis took both **prize** ships to Goletta, his base in Tunisia, north Africa. For him, the greatest prize of all was the prisoners. The captured Christians became galley **slaves**, and they were forced to row the ships of their Muslim masters.

7

Pirates of the Mediterranean: 1500–1650

The Mediterranean Sea was the haunt of pirates long before Aruj Reis.

Pirates **plundered** ships and captured men, women and children, who they sold as slaves or held hostage. The pirates' most famous hostage was Julius Caesar. He was captured in 75 BC and held for 38 days, until a **ransom** was paid for his release. Caesar returned to the pirates' den with help and executed them. The Mediterranean became a safer sea for travellers and merchants.

Spain

Italy

Morocco

Mediterranean Sea

Barbary Coast

Algiers

Tunis

⬆ *The Barbary Coast – a region along the coast of north Africa – was home to Muslim corsairs between about 1500 and 1650.*

Piracy returned to the Mediterranean in the AD 800s, when Muslim pirates from north Africa and eastern Spain began to raid Christian ships and towns. It was the start of a **holy war** that lasted for several hundred years. By about 1300, the worst of the fighting was over. Then, in the 1500s, Muslim pirates began to attack Christian ships and towns again, and a new period of Mediterranean piracy began. This was when the Barbarossa brothers – Aruj and Hizir Reis – were active.

SHIVER ME TIMBERS!

Muslim pirates were usually given the title 'reis' by their men. It is an Arabic word meaning 'captain' or 'commander'.

ROGUES' GALLERY

Uluj Ali Reis
Active as a pirate
1550s–1587

**Aruj Reis,
'Barbarossa'**
Active as a pirate
1500–1518

**Hizir Reis,
'Barbarossa'**
Active as a pirate
1500–1544

Hamidou Reis
Active as a pirate
1790–1815

John Ward
Active as a pirate
1600–1623

Murat Reis
Active as a pirate
c.1565–1638

The Barbary Coast

For about 150 years from 1500 to 1650, the coast of north Africa was a safe haven for Muslim pirates.

Their realm stretched for hundreds of kilometres, eastwards from modern-day Algeria to Libya. Although north Africa is now made up of countries, it was once a collection of **city-states** ruled by Muslim princes. The states were Tripoli, Tunis, Algiers and Morocco. Europeans called the region the **Barbary Coast**, and the raiders who sailed out from its many ports were Barbary **corsairs**.

⬆ *A Christian priest buys back Christian slaves from their Muslim masters.*

Corsair or privateer?

Corsair and privateer mean the same thing – raiders acting with the permission of their rulers. Corsair is for raiders from the north African or Barbary Coast, as well as France. Privateer is for raiders from Europe.

The Barbarossa brothers were amongst the first corsairs to sail from the ports of the Barbary Coast. As Muslim corsairs, they had permission from their city-states to raid non-Muslim targets – Christian towns and ships. As long as they did not break this basic rule and begin to attack their own people, Muslim corsairs believed that they were doing nothing wrong. Christians and other non-Muslims didn't see it this way at all. To their way of thinking, the Barbarossas, and men like them, were nothing more than pirates.

If a captured Christian attempted to escape, the punishment was severe.

A corsair galley

Galleys were a common sight on the Mediterranean Sea, where they were used as merchant ships, warships and pirate ships.

All galleys were long, narrow **vessels** that sat low in the water. In the early 1500s, the galleys used by merchants to transport goods and people were up to 55 metres in length, while war galleys were about 47 metres in length.

Barbary corsairs preferred smaller galleys, known as **galiots**. They were about half the size of a merchant galley and were fast and easy to move around. Along each side of a galley was a row of oars. The oars were lined up in pairs, one on each side of the ship. On a corsair galley, each oar was pulled by two men. They were slaves or prisoners who were forced to work as rowers.

Main sail

Swivel gun

Deck gun

Ram

Anchor

It was their back-breaking effort that moved the galley through the water. At dash speed, a good crew could row 1.5 kilometres in six or seven minutes. They could keep this speed up for about 20 minutes, after which they would feel tired and the galley slowed down. It wasn't all hard work, though. On windy days, **sails** were used to move a galley along.

Captain's quarters

Oar

Water cask

Corsair galley at a glance

Length: 27 metres

Width: 3 metres

Oars: 16 to 20 pairs (32 to 40 oars)

Oar length: 4.5 metres

Oarsmen: 64 to 80

Corsairs: Up to 60

Cruising speed: 4 knots (8 kilometres an hour)

Dash speed: 8 knots (15 kilometres an hour)

Galley slaves

Taking prisoners was part of piracy in the Mediterranean Sea.

Christian pirates took Muslims, and Muslim pirates took Christians, just as Aruj Reis did when he captured the Pope's galleys. Both sides turned their prisoners into slaves, and many were forced to work as 'human machines' that rowed the galleys of their masters.

SHIVER ME TIMBERS!

On 20 June 1631, the village of Baltimore, on the south coast of Ireland, was raided by Barbary pirates. More than 100 villagers were taken to north Africa and became slaves. In the 1600s, people were also snatched by corsairs from English towns in Devon and Cornwall.

◄ *Banks of Christian prisoners rowing a Muslim galley. The captain threatened them with harsh punishment if they stopped working.*

14

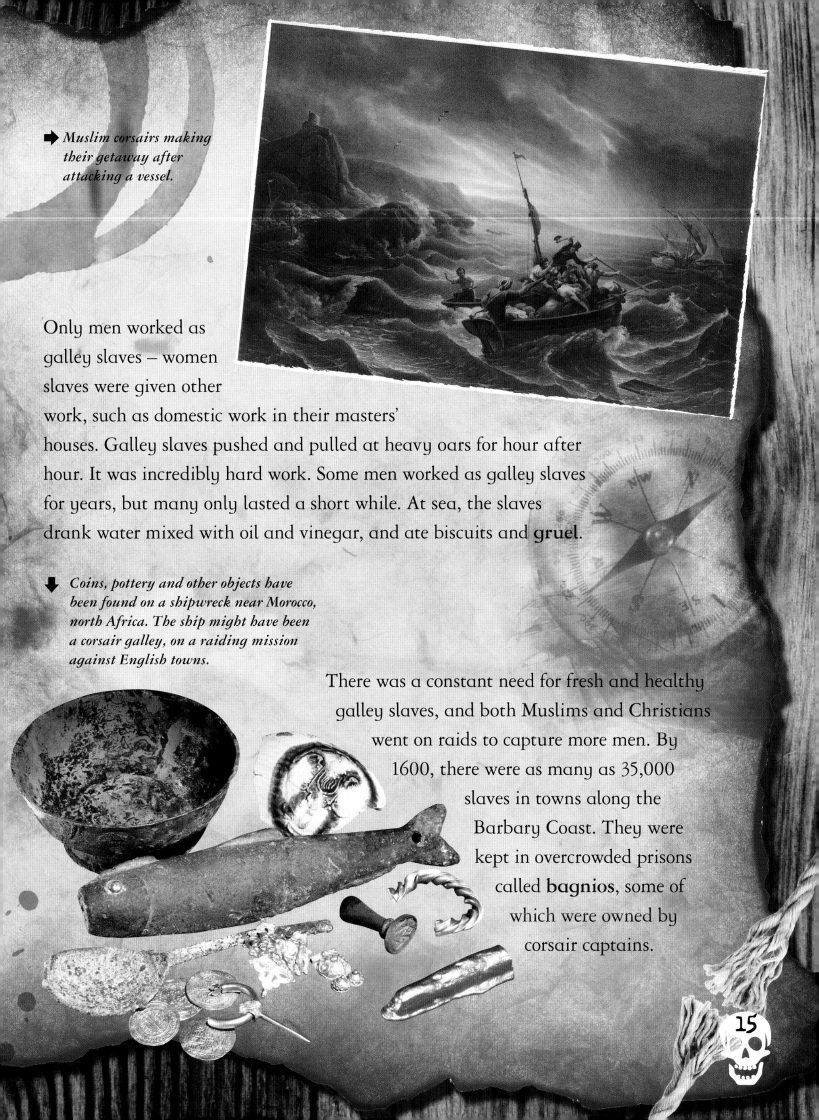

➡ *Muslim corsairs making their getaway after attacking a vessel.*

Only men worked as galley slaves – women slaves were given other work, such as domestic work in their masters' houses. Galley slaves pushed and pulled at heavy oars for hour after hour. It was incredibly hard work. Some men worked as galley slaves for years, but many only lasted a short while. At sea, the slaves drank water mixed with oil and vinegar, and ate biscuits and **gruel**.

⬇ *Coins, pottery and other objects have been found on a shipwreck near Morocco, north Africa. The ship might have been a corsair galley, on a raiding mission against English towns.*

There was a constant need for fresh and healthy galley slaves, and both Muslims and Christians went on raids to capture more men. By 1600, there were as many as 35,000 slaves in towns along the Barbary Coast. They were kept in overcrowded prisons called **bagnios**, some of which were owned by corsair captains.

15

Attacked by corsairs

Corsair captains built up fleets of galleys. By 1512, Aruj Reis commanded 12 galleys and an army of several hundred men.

He would have needed at least 1000 slaves to row his galleys, with many more held in reserve in the slave prisons of north Africa.

A corsair sword had a curved blade and is known as a scimitar.

At first, Barbary corsairs only attacked vessels in the Mediterranean Sea, but by the 1600s, they were menacing ships and towns far away from their north African bases. Raids were carried out as far away as Britain, Ireland and even Iceland.

A corsair galley had one small **cannon** at the very front. In an attack, the galley pointed towards its enemy, and when it was within range, the cannon was fired. By the time the gun was ready to fire again, the galley was too close to its enemy. At this point, the galley's soldiers climbed on board the enemy ship. They fought hand-to-hand, and when the fighting was over, the enemy ship and its crew had become the corsairs' prize.

▼ *Corsair galleys in battle against larger sailing ships from Europe.*

SHIVER ME TIMBERS!

In just seven years, between 1609 and 1616, Barbary corsairs captured 466 ships from around the coast of Britain, and thousands of men were taken prisoner.

17

Aruj Reis:
the one-armed corsair

Aruj Reis was the first in his family to embark on a life of piracy. He was a small man with a red beard and red hair.

His men called him 'Baba Aruj', which meant 'Father Aruj', but his Christian enemies called him 'Barbarossa', which meant 'Red Beard'.

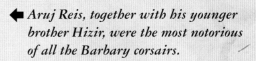

Aruj Reis,
known as 'Barbarossa'

Born: 1470s, on the island of Lesbos, Greece

Died: 1518, at Oran, Algeria

Occupation: Corsair

◄ *Aruj Reis, together with his younger brother Hizir, were the most notorious of all the Barbary corsairs.*

In the late 1400s, Aruj attacked ships in the eastern Mediterranean. In one attack, he was captured by Christians and became one of their galley slaves. An Egyptian prince paid for Aruj to be set free, after which he settled on the Barbary Coast with his younger brother, Hizir. They made Tunisia their base, before moving west to a new base in Algeria.

Aruj raided Christian ships in the western Mediterranean. His most daring raid was in 1504, when he captured a pair of galleys owned by the Pope. The following year, he seized a Spanish warship with 500 soldiers. In 1512, during an attack on a Spanish fort in Algeria, Aruj lost his left arm. From then on, he wanted revenge against the Spanish, but in 1518, during a battle on the outskirts of Oran, he was killed by soldiers sent by the King of Spain.

SHIVER ME TIMBERS!

In 1516, Aruj overthrew the ruler of Algiers and declared himself the new *sultan*, or prince.

◀ *Led by Aruj Reis, corsairs board the galley of Pope Julius II. The crew became his prisoners, and were taken to Tunisia, north Africa, where they began their new lives as galley slaves.*

John Ward: the pirate who changed sides

Not all Barbary corsairs were born as Muslims. Some were Christian pirates who converted to Islam.

John Ward was an English pirate who began his pirate career raiding ships in the Caribbean. In about 1604, he fled to the Mediterranean, where he carried on plundering ships.

SHIVER ME TIMBERS!

A traveller from Scotland visited Ward when he was an old man. He discovered that Ward had a hobby – raising chickens. He kept the eggs warm in camel dung!

◄ Pirates from the Barbary Coast capture slaves on the north Mediterranean coast.

John Ward,
known as 'Yusuf Reis'

Born: c.1553

Died: 1623, of plague, in Tunis

Occupation: Pirate

It wasn't long before Ward came to the attention of Barbary corsairs, and by 1606 he had found a safe haven among them at Tunis. From there, he raided European ships carrying spices and gold. In one raid, Ward seized cargo worth £100,000, which he sold to Osman Bey, the ruler of Tunis, for £20,000. In return, Bey let Ward use his port. It was a small price to pay for his protection.

⬇ *Ward used his own money to buy freedom for English slaves held prisoner in north Africa.*

In 1610, Ward converted to Islam. He took the name Yusuf Reis, although many Muslims called him 'Captain Wardiyya'. He freed English slaves held in corsair prisons, and in England he was celebrated in songs. There was even a play written about him called *A Christian Turn'd Turk*. In the play, he was killed off at the end and his body was thrown into the sea. The real John Ward lived a life of luxury in Tunis and was waited on by English servants!

21

Hizir Reis: the gift of God

Like his elder brother Aruj, Hizir Reis also had striking red hair and a red beard.

He was an educated man who spoke all the main Mediterranean languages – Greek, Arabic, Spanish, Italian and French.

↑ *Commanded by Hizir Reis, the Ottoman (Turkish) navy was the strongest force in the eastern Mediterranean, until losing the Battle of Lepanto in 1571.*

SHIVER ME TIMBERS!

In 1529, Hizir used a fleet of 36 galleys to transport 70,000 Muslims from Spain to north Africa. It took seven trips to move them all.

After his brother's death in 1518, Hizir became the leader of the family's fleet of galleys. He continued the fight against Spain that his brother had begun. Hizir attacked Spain's possessions on the north African coast, and his galleys forced a Spanish fleet to retreat.

As Hizir grew in power, he was made ruler of the Barbary city-states, and in 1533 he was put in charge of the Ottoman (Turkish) navy. Two years later, he led a fleet of galleys to the Spanish island of Majorca. He looted the island and took 6000 prisoners. In further raids, he attacked southern Italy and France, and defeated fleets of galleys sent by Spain, the Pope and the cities of Italy.

↑ *The battle flag of Hizir Reis. The Arabic writing at the top says, 'Mohammed! Reveal good news to the believers that the conquest is soon'.*

◄ *In 1530, Hizir and his crew raided Tunis, capturing many slaves.*

Hizir's success as a sea captain made the Ottoman navy the strongest force in the Mediterranean and he was given the title 'Khayr-al-Din', which meant 'the gift of God'.

Hizir Reis,
known as 'Barbarossa'

Born: c.1470s, on the island of Lesbos, Greece

Died: 1546, at Istanbul, Turkey

Occupation: Corsair and naval commander

23

Murat Reis: Captain of the Sea

After being captured by a Barbary corsair when he was a teenager, he took the Muslim name 'Murat'.

Murat became a corsair captain, and as his attacks against Christian ships and towns increased, he gained a reputation as a powerful Muslim warrior. He was also very cunning.

⬇ *Murat fought in the Battle of Lepanto in 1571. He was overpowered, along with the rest of the Ottoman navy by a stronger Christian force.*

SHIVER ME TIMBERS!

Murat died while attacking the city of Vlore, Albania. He was probably about 100 years old at the time!

Murat Reis

Born: c.1534, in Albania

Died: 1638, fighting in Albania

Occupation: Corsair and naval commander

When his ships attacked, he lowered the masts of his smaller galleys. Murat towed the little galleys behind his bigger ones, and because they were low in the water, they were hard to see. This tricked his enemy into thinking he had only a few ships and men.

Murat Reis approached a victim with care, sneaking up on a ship then mounting a sudden, surprise attack.

Murat was the first Barbary corsair to venture out of the Mediterranean Sea. In 1586, he sailed through the Strait of Gibraltar – the narrow passage between Spain and north Africa – and into the Atlantic Ocean. He headed for the Canary Islands, off the coast of west Africa, and raided Lanzarote. Murat took the Spanish governor prisoner and only let him go after he was paid a large sum of money. In 1578, Murat was given the title 'Captain of the Sea'.

Uluj Ali Reis:
galley slave to sea captain

Thousands of Christian slaves rowed galleys for Muslim corsairs. Almost nothing is known about them, except for one. His name was Giovanni Dionigi.

He lived in southern Italy and probably expected to become a fisherman, like his father. However, in 1536, when he was about 16 years old, he was captured by a Muslim raider and began working as a rower on a Muslim galley.

SHIVER ME TIMBERS!

Muslims and Christians signed a **peace treaty** in 1577. It put an end to their holy war, but it did not stamp out piracy. In fact, more pirates, both Muslim and Christian, began to sail in the Mediterranean Sea than ever before.

It is believed that Giovanni Dionigi fell in love with his captor's daughter. In order to marry her, he converted to Islam and changed his name to Uluj Ali. From then on, he was a free man and decided to fight on the side of the corsairs.

◄ *Uluj Ali was a great leader and fought many battles, including the Battle of Lepanto in 1571.*

Uluj Ali became a leading corsair. He commanded a fleet of galleys, and led attacks against Spain and Italy. In 1571, he fought in the Battle of Lepanto, off the west coast of Greece. For five hours, about 300 Muslim galleys battled 200 Christian war galleys. Although the Muslim force was defeated, Uluj Ali fought bravely and led some ships to safety. After this, he became commander-in-chief of the Ottoman (Turkish) navy, and spent the rest of his life protecting the Barbary Coast from Christian attacks.

Uluj Ali

Born: c.1520, in Italy

Died: 1587, in Istanbul, Turkey

Occupation: Corsair and naval commander

▼ *The Battle of Lepanto lasted for about five hours. The Ottoman (Turkish) navy was defeated by a Christian force from Spain and Italy. It was the last major sea battle fought by galleys.*

Captured crew

The golden age of Barbary corsairs ended around 1650 – but this did not mean the Mediterranean was then safe for all ships.

The pirates of the Barbary city-states demanded **protection money** from ships, and in return they promised to leave merchant ships alone. In 1800, the ruler of Tripoli asked for more money, and the US government decided to send a fleet of warships to fight the pirates. At first, all went well. The US warships **blockaded** Tripoli, stopping pirates from entering and leaving the port.

◄ *The* Philadelphia *burning in the harbour at Tripoli, after the raid by Stephen Decatur.*

More warships were sent in 1803. One of them was the *Philadelphia*, but as it chased an enemy vessel, it became stuck close to the shores of Tripoli. The crew of 300 was taken prisoner. The pirates claimed the warship as their prize, and began changing it for their own use.

➡ *Lieutenant Stephen Decatur (in uniform, lying on the deck) fights the crew of a gunboat from Tripoli.*

SHIVER ME TIMBERS!

After the war ended, the USA no longer paid protection money to the state of Tripoli – but other nations did.

Then, in a daring raid led by Lieutenant Stephen Decatur in 1804, a group of US seamen sneaked on board the *Philadelphia* and started a fire that sank the ship. After the destruction of the *Philadelphia*, the crew was released in exchange for prisoners held by the USA. A peace treaty was signed by both sides in 1805.

Hamidou Reis: last of the corsairs

The threat from Barbary corsairs finally ended in 1815.

A few years before, Hamidou Reis had made Algiers his base for raids against foreign ships. Between 1797 and 1800, he seized 19 ships and posed a serious problem in the western Mediterranean. Unlike his **ancestors**, Hamidou did not use galleys. Instead, he used ships with sails, and his flagship was armed with 44 cannon and carried a crew of 400 men.

Hamidou Reis

Born: date not known, in Algeria

Died: 1815, off the coast of Spain

Occupation: Corsair

In battle, Hamidou showed his cunning. In 1802, he raised the British flag on his ship. As he closed in on a Portuguese vessel, they thought a friend was approaching. It was a similar trick to the one used by Aruj Reis 300 years earlier, when he disguised his men in the clothes of his captives. Hamidou took the Portuguese ship, and went on to capture ships from Denmark, Sweden, Holland, Spain, Italy, Greece and America.

⬆ *The death of Hamidou Reis, hit by a cannon ball and cut in two.*

⬇ *British and Dutch ships bombarded Algiers, capital of Algeria, on 27 August 1816. After the attack, about 3000 slaves were set free.*

In 1815, Hamidou was spotted off the coast of Spain by a US warship. The Americans tricked him by using his own tactic of flying the British flag, and the corsair let them approach. In the battle that followed, Hamidou was killed by a US cannon ball.

Francis Drake

and the Sea Rovers of the Spanish Main

CONTENTS

Pirate attack!

In 1579, English sea captain Francis Drake was sailing in the Pacific Ocean in his ship the Golden Hind.

Drake was following orders given to him by Queen Elizabeth I – to explore the Pacific (west) coast of South America and raid Spanish ships and settlements. Drake boasted that "all the ships in the Pacific were in his power", and when he learned the Spanish **treasure ship** the *Cacafuego* had sailed from Peru loaded with gold, silver and jewels, it became his target.

➡ *Despite being much bigger than the* Golden Hind, *the* Cacafuego *was easily captured by Francis Drake. It was an act that made him a pirate to the Spanish, but a national hero to the English.*

34

After a long chase, Drake caught up with the *Cacafuego*. The captain refused to surrender, so the English opened fire. **Chain shot** felled the **mizzen mast**, arrows rained down, and 40 of Drake's men went on board.

The *Cacafuego* was soon in Drake's hands, together with a fortune in treasure. There was so much **booty** that it took three days to move it onto the *Golden Hind*. The haul included 13 chests of silver *reales* (Spanish coins), 25 tonnes of silver bars, 36 kilograms of gold and a large quantity of jewellery.

Pirates of the Spanish Main: 1550–1600

In the 1500s, Spain controlled much of Central America, the northern coast of South America and many of the islands in the Caribbean.

This vast area became part of the Spanish Empire. It was rich in silver, gold and gems, which were brought to Spain by fleets of **merchant ships**. The Spaniards had several names for their overseas territory, one of which was New Spain. Their English and French rivals had their own name for it – the **Spanish Main**.

⬇ *Spain's empire in the Americas became known as the 'Spanish Main'. It covered a large area of land and sea, and offered rich pickings to pirates.*

North America

Caribbean Islands

Caribbean Sea

South America

From about 1550 to 1600, the Spanish Main was the haunt of 'sea dogs' from England, France and the Netherlands. Many, such as Francis Drake, went there with permission from their governments to **plunder** Spain's treasure **fleets** and settlements. They thought of themselves as **privateers**, but to the Spaniards they were pirates. There was a fortune to be had by both sides. Spain looted the region's treasures and, in turn, the privateers – or pirates – took the treasure from the Spaniards.

ROGUES' GALLERY

Francis Drake
Active as a privateer and pirate
1570–1596

John Hawkins
Active as a privateer and pirate
1562–1595

Richard Grenville
Active as a privateer and pirate
1586–1591

Jean Bontemps
Active as a privateer and pirate
1567–1570

Thomas Cavendish
Active as a privateer and pirate
1586–1592

Jean Fleury
Active as a privateer and pirate
1523–1527

37

Privateers and pirates

When Francis Drake captured the Spanish treasure galleon the Cacafuego in 1579, the Spanish called him a pirate.

Drake did not think of himself as a pirate at all. This was because he had orders from Queen Elizabeth I of England to raid ships and towns that belonged to England's enemy. Drake was, to the English, a privateer. Whereas a pirate worked for himself and raided any ship he liked, a privateer worked for his country and only attacked his country's enemies. Drake was one of many English, French and Dutch privateers who sailed to the Spanish Main in search of treasure for themselves and their rulers.

⬆ The Great Seal of Queen Elizabeth I was used to seal government documents, such as a Letter of Marque issued to a privateer. The seal showed the document was official.

⬅ For much of her reign (1558–1603), Queen Elizabeth I of England was at war with Spain. She supported English privateers, giving them permission to attack Spanish ships and towns.

Privateers were issued with Letters of Marque by their rulers. The letters were licences that gave them permission to raid enemy ships and towns. As they were working for their rulers, privateers agreed to give them the valuables they seized. In return, they were allowed to keep a share of the **loot** for themselves.

▼ *The English government kept its share of treasure taken by privateers at the Tower of London – a fortress close to the centre of England's capital city.*

SHIVER ME TIMBERS!

During the reign of Queen Elizabeth I, many English sea dogs did not get a privateering licence. Francis Drake was one of them. He carried out his raids knowing that he had the full support of his queen, whether he had a licence from her or not!

Treasure galleons

Treasure from the Spanish Main was taken to Spain by cargo ships known as galleons.

They were the main ocean-going ships of the day, with three masts, square sails and several decks. Below the waterline were the cargo decks, where goods were stored in crates and barrels. Gold, silver and jewels were kept in the treasure hold, which was the ship's strongroom.

Foremast

Forecastle

Bowsprit

Prow

At each end of a galleon was a tall section known as a **castle**. The **forecastle** was at the bow, or front, and the **sterncastle** was at the stern, or rear. The castles were fighting platforms where soldiers shot at their enemy with arrows and crossbow bolts.

Gunport

Galleon at a glance

Length: 30 to 45 metres

Width: 12 to 15 metres

Weight: 200 to 1000 tonnes

Speed: 8 knots
(15 kilometres an hour)

Crew: Up to 200

Cannon: 20 to 50

With towering castles, high sides and many guns, galleons were top-heavy ships. They were difficult to manoeuvre and were easily rocked by the sea. Many galleons were lost in storms and some were picked off by pirates.

Ship's lantern

Mizzenmast

Sterncastle

Mainmast

Gundeck

Powder and shot store

Treasure hold

⬆ A galleon was designed to carry goods, from everyday items to treasure. It was stored on the ship's cargo decks.

41

As pirates set about plundering the Spanish Main, Spain looked for ways to protect its ships and settlements.

Fortresses were built to guard ports and ships at anchor, but something else had to be done to protect ships on the open sea. From the 1520s, Spanish galleons heading home to Spain began sailing in fleets, guarded by warships. There could be 20 or more treasure galleons in a fleet, protected by heavily armed **escort ships**.

➡ *Richard Grenville and his crew attack the* Revenge *in 1591. They were outnumbered, so he surrendered. He died two days later.*

↑ *Escorted by warships, Spain's treasure fleets crossed the Atlantic Ocean, taking their valuable cargoes to Spain.*

The Spanish treasure ships were loaded with silver from Mexico and Peru, gold from Ecuador, emeralds from Colombia, and pearls from Venezuela. After collecting their cargoes, the ships met up at Havana, Cuba, then began the long voyage across the Atlantic Ocean. It was difficult for a pirate ship to attack the fleet, as it was out-numbered and out-gunned. All it could hope for was for one of the galleons to become separated from the fleet, as happened in 1585 when Richard Grenville captured the *Santa Maria*, with treasure worth at least £50,000.

SHIVER ME TIMBERS!

In just four years, between 1596 and 1600, Spanish ships carried treasure worth more than 34 million **pesos** to Spain — about £516 million today.

43

Jean Fleury: Atlantic raider

Pirates on both sides of the Atlantic Ocean dreamed of capturing a Spanish treasure ship.

For the French pirate Jean Fleury, his dream came true in 1523. When he spotted three Spanish galleons off the Azores (a group of islands in the mid-Atlantic Ocean), he began his attack. He knew they were on the final leg of the voyage home to Spain, but had no idea what they were carrying.

↑ *Aztec goldsmiths crafted beautiful objects, such as this mask. Spaniards wanted the Aztecs' gold, which they melted down and turned into ingots and coins.*

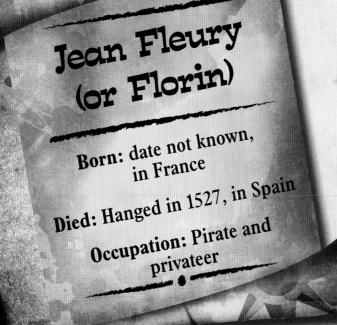

Jean Fleury (or Florin)

Born: date not known, in France

Died: Hanged in 1527, in Spain

Occupation: Pirate and privateer

After a chase and then a battle off the coast of southern Portugal, Fleury captured two of the galleons. He could scarcely believe his luck at what he found on board. The ships were carrying treasure taken from Montezuma, the last Aztec ruler of Mexico.

It was a massive haul of gold ingots, gold dust, pearls, emeralds and jewellery. Montezuma's treasure had been on its way to the king of Spain. In 1527, Fleury was captured and sold to the king, who promptly had him executed.

⬇ *No one was more surprised at the quantity of treasure than Jean Fleury.*

SHIVER ME TIMBERS!

Fleury's haul also included live parrots and jaguars, and several tonnes of sugar, which was as valuable as gold.

Doubloons and pieces of eight

In 1545, Spanish explorers discovered that a mountain at Potosí, Bolivia, contained a huge amount of valuable silver.

The Spanish claimed the silver for themselves and forced local people to dig it out. Before the silver was taken to Spain, it was cast into heavy ingots or struck into coins.

SHIVER ME TIMBERS!

In 1644, Spanish pieces of eight were worth four shillings and sixpence each in England (22.5p). In today's money, that is about £15.

A treasure chest used by the Spanish to transport silver. It was made of wood bound with iron, and was locked with padlocks.

◄ *Safety in numbers.
When Spain's treasure
fleet sailed for home, it
was escorted by warships.
If a storm scattered the
fleet, the treasure galleons
became vulnerable
to attack.*

*▲ A Spanish silver peso, known
to pirates as a piece of eight.*

Spaniards called their silver coins pesos or *reales*.
Each one had the number eight on it, meaning it
was worth eight *reales*. Pirates had their own name for
them – pieces of eight. The most valuable Spanish coins
were made from gold, which the Spaniards mined in
Colombia and Mexico. The gold coin was the eight
escudo piece, which pirates called a **doubloon**.

It has been worked out that the treasure on a Spanish
treasure ship was made up of about 80 percent silver
and 20 percent gold. A pirate who managed to grab
just a handful of doubloons or pieces of eight was a rich
man, but imagine how much richer he would be if he
captured a treasure ship and all of its treasure!

47

John Hawkins: slave trader

The Spanish wanted to control the traders who took goods to the Spanish Main. The Spanish Main was their territory, so they decided who to trade with.

Although Spain and England were enemies, it was still possible for English merchants to trade with the Spanish, but the traders had to have permission from the Spanish government. John Hawkins did not have permission, but he still traded with Spain's **colonies** in the Spanish Main.

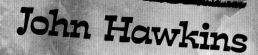

John Hawkins

Born: 1532, in England

Died: 1595, off the coast of Puerto Rico

Occupation: Privateer, pirate, slave trader and naval commander

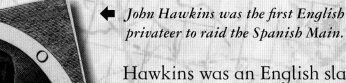
John Hawkins was the first English privateer to raid the Spanish Main.

Hawkins was an English slave trader. He gathered his first human cargo in 1562, raiding Portuguese slave ships off the coast of west Africa. By raiding Portuguese ships, he became a pirate. He crossed the Atlantic Ocean and sold the 300 African slaves to Spanish settlers on the island of Hispaniola, in return for gold, silver and pearls. Hawkins made another slave-trading voyage in 1564, again with hundreds of Africans seized from the Portuguese. It was just as successful.

↑ The Jesus of Lubeck *was a royal ship loaned to Hawkins by Queen Elizabeth I. It was a large, heavy ship, which Hawkins used to carry African slaves.*

Hawkins was not so lucky on his next voyage. In 1568, his fleet of six ships was attacked at the port of San Juan de Ulúa, Mexico, by Spanish galleons. Only two ships escaped – the *Minion*, commanded by Hawkins, and the *Judith*, commanded by his cousin, Francis Drake.

SHIVER ME TIMBERS!

Hawkins almost did not make it back to England. The *Minion* was a leaky ship with little food on board. Of the 100 crew members, only about 15 came home. They survived by eating rats and parrots.

Privateer Weapons

A privateer's main weapon was their ship. It was usually a warship, smaller than a Spanish galleon, and armed with about 20 guns of various sizes.

There were large **cannon** that blasted enemy ships and ports with heavy cannonballs, and smaller **swivel guns** that fired **grapeshot** at other crews.

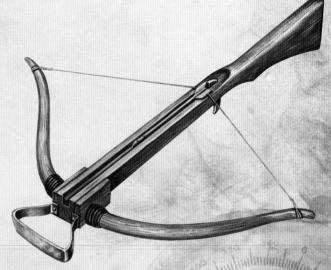

▲ *A crossbow fired a short arrow called a bolt, which had a metal point.*

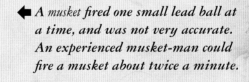

◄ *A musket fired one small lead ball at a time, and was not very accurate. An experienced musket-man could fire a musket about twice a minute.*

For fighting at closer range, the crew used crossbows and firearms called muskets. These were guns with long barrels that fired balls of solid lead about 82 metres. If the fighting spread onto the ship, **rapiers**, daggers and half-pikes were used in hand-to-hand combat. A **pike** was a pole with a sharp metal point at the end, used for jabbing.

For fighting on land, privateers used full-length pikes and **halberds**. A full pike measured up to 5.5 metres long, and a halberd was a spiked axe at the end of a pole. Some men wore metal armour on their chests and backs, but most protected themselves with **jerkins** – jackets made from padded leather.

⬆ *Armed with swords, halberds and half-pikes, a group of privateers raid a settlement in search of plunder.*

SHIVER ME TIMBERS!

Cannonballs were made from solid stone or iron. The smallest were about the size of tennis balls, and weighed about 0.45 kilograms. The biggest were a little smaller than footballs and weighed about 29 kilograms.

Francis Drake: the Queen's pirate

Francis Drake was the most famous of the English sea dogs in the Spanish Main.

Drake first ventured to the Main on slave-trading expeditions led by his cousin John Hawkins. After the battle with the Spanish that destroyed the English fleet in 1568, Drake wanted his revenge.

◄ *Queen Elizabeth I called Francis Drake 'my pirate'. In 1581, she went on board the* Golden Hind *and knighted him. From then on, he was Sir Francis Drake.*

Between 1570 and 1573, Drake attacked many Spanish ships and ports. In February 1573, he tried to capture a convoy of silver being carried to the waiting Spanish treasure ships. The attack failed. He tried again later that year, and took so much gold and silver that it was impossible to carry it all away, so he only took the gold. In England, Drake was greeted as a hero, and gained the support of Queen Elizabeth I.

In 1577, Drake sailed to the Main in the *Golden Hind*, with orders from the Queen to plunder Spanish property. It was his most famous voyage and it lasted three years. In March 1579, Drake captured the treasure ship *Cacafuego*, then sailed for England. He took the long way home, and ended up sailing right around the world!

Francis Drake

Born: 1540, in England

Died: 1596, in the harbour at Porto Bello, Jamaica

Occupation: Privateer, pirate, sea captain and explorer

◀ *Francis Drake was the first Englishman to sail around the world. The voyage of the* Golden Hind *lasted three years, from 1577 to 1580.*

The Golden Hind

The little ship that took Francis Drake to success in the Spanish Main, and then went on to circumnavigate the world, was originally called the *Pelican*.

It sailed from Plymouth, England, in December 1577. Eight months later, as Drake prepared to sail around the tip of South America, he renamed the ship the *Golden Hind*.

Golden Hind at a glance

Length: 21 metres

Width: 6 metres

Weight: 100 tonnes

Speed: 8 knots (15 kilometres an hour)

Crew: 80

Cannon: 18

The *Golden Hind* was a warship, smaller than a Spanish galleon. Unlike bulky galleons, which had high sides and high-rise castles at each end, the *Golden Hind* was lower and sleeker. It could sail faster than a galleon and it was easier to handle.

SHIVER ME TIMBERS!

Today, all that remains of the *Golden Hind* is an oak chair made from its timber. It is in the Bodleian Library, Oxford, England.

◄ *Drake renamed the* Pelican *the* Golden Hind *in honour of Sir Christopher Hatton, a politician who had helped pay for Drake's voyage. Hatton's coat of arms included a golden hind (a female deer), which gave Drake the idea.*

The *Golden Hind* was the first English ship to sail around the world, and it became every bit as famous as the captain. The ship was put on display at Deptford, near London, England, which is where Queen Elizabeth I boarded it to knight Francis Drake in 1581. By the late 1600s, the *Golden Hind* had fallen into a poor state. The rotten timbers were beyond repair, and it was broken up for scrap.

Drake's final voyage

Francis Drake sailed to the Spanish Main for the last time in 1595. It was also John Hawkins' last voyage.

The two cousins shared command of the expedition. They took 26 ships and 2500 men. The plan was to capture Spanish treasure – but it did not work out. Drake and Hawkins argued from the start. Drake wanted to attack the Canary Islands, off the coast of north Africa, but Hawkins did not. Drake got his way, but the attack failed and some of his men were taken prisoner. They told the Spaniards about Drake's plan to raid the Spanish Main.

By the time the fleet reached the Main, the Spaniards were ready for the English. Drake wanted to attack Puerto Rico straightaway, but Hawkins thought it would be better to wait. Hawkins was ill, and while the ships were at anchor, he died.

SHIVER ME TIMBERS!

Drake had ordered his men to bury him on dry land. They ignored him. Instead, his body was put into a lead coffin and was buried at sea, the day after he died.

56

Drake went ahead with the attack, but the Spaniards fought him off. After that, he looked in other places for treasure, without much luck. A disease called **dysentery** killed many of his men, and in January 1596, Drake caught it and died. With both their leaders now dead, the fleet set sail and headed back to England.

▼ *The Spanish fortress at Puerto Rico was heavily armed, and Drake's attack was a failure.*

Jean Bontemps: the fair weather man

Pirates from France and Holland also sailed the Spanish Main.

One was Jean Bontemps – a nickname meaning 'good weather'. He came from France, and in 1567, sailed to west Africa and collected human cargo.

Bontemps tried to sell the slaves in Venezuela, but the Spanish settlers refused to trade with him. He sailed to Colombia, and on the way, seized a Spanish treasure galleon.

Jean Bontemps

Born: not known, in France

Died: 1570, in action at Curaçao

Occupation: Pirate

➡ *African slaves shipped across the Atlantic in the 1500s were sold to Spanish landowners in the Spanish Main.*

Bontemps managed to sell the slaves in Colombia, but only because he threatened to kill the slaves if the Colombians did not trade with him. On the return journey to France, Bontemps raided Spanish towns on Hispaniola and captured several ships. It had been a profitable voyage for him, but his luck did not last.

In 1572, Bontemps raided the Spanish island of Curaçao, off the north coast of Venezuela. About 70 men took part in the attack, but as it was pouring with rain, the **gunpowder** for their guns became damp and they did not work. Bontemps was killed. For once, he had not lived up to his nickname – the weather had helped him to get killed.

◄ *Jean Bontemps was struck in the throat by an arrow and killed.*

William Kidd

and the
Pirates of the Indian Ocean

CONTENTS

Pirate attack!

William Kidd was supposed to be hunting pirates in the Indian Ocean, but he became a pirate himself.

As he turned the *Adventure Galley* towards the large **merchant ship** sailing near the west coast of India, he was about to seize the greatest **prize** of his pirating career.

It was January 1698, and the *Adventure Galley*, despite her rotten and leaky hull, was soon upon the *Quedah Merchant*. As she closed in, Kidd raised French flags. It was an old trick, which the captain of the *Quedah Merchant* fell for – the false flags made him think that Kidd's ship was friendly. Kidd went aboard the *Quedah Merchant* without a struggle, and told its captain that he was claiming the ship as his prize. In the ship's hold was a valuable **cargo** of silk, **calico**, sugar, iron, guns and gold coins.

◄ *William Kidd's* Adventure Galley *closes in on the* Quedah Merchant, *an Indian trading ship. Kidd sold most of the cargo for £7000 and kept the captured ship for himself.*

After selling most of the cargo at a port in India, Kidd sailed the *Quedah Merchant* to the pirate **haven** of Madagascar, where he fitted it out with **cannon** from the *Adventure Galley*. He renamed the ship the *Adventure Prize* and it became his new **flagship**.

63

Pirates of the Indian Ocean: 1690–1720

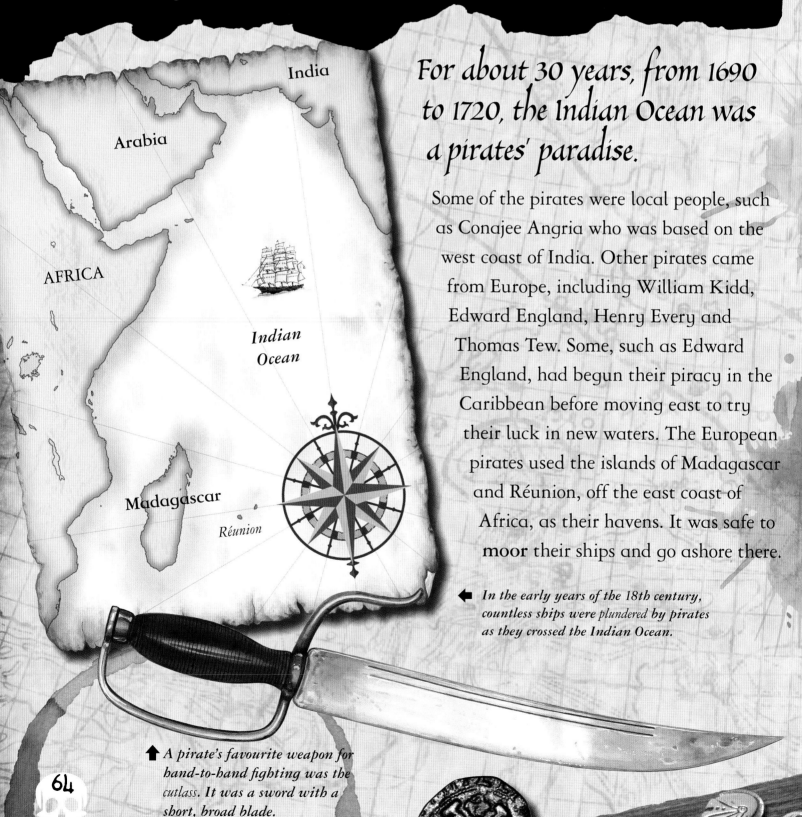

India

Arabia

AFRICA

Indian Ocean

Madagascar

Réunion

For about 30 years, from 1690 to 1720, the Indian Ocean was a pirates' paradise.

Some of the pirates were local people, such as Conajee Angria who was based on the west coast of India. Other pirates came from Europe, including William Kidd, Edward England, Henry Every and Thomas Tew. Some, such as Edward England, had begun their piracy in the Caribbean before moving east to try their luck in new waters. The European pirates used the islands of Madagascar and Réunion, off the east coast of Africa, as their havens. It was safe to **moor** their ships and go ashore there.

◀ *In the early years of the 18th century, countless ships were plundered by pirates as they crossed the Indian Ocean.*

▲ *A pirate's favourite weapon for hand-to-hand fighting was the cutlass. It was a sword with a short, broad blade.*

ROGUES' GALLERY

Henry Every
Active as a pirate
1692–1695

Thomas Tew
Active as a pirate
1692–1695

Edward England
Active as a pirate
1717–1720

SHIVER ME TIMBERS!

Pirates of the Indian Ocean were probably the most successful pirates in history. When it came to sharing out the **loot**, each man probably received about £1000. Pirates in the Caribbean were lucky to get £20!

William Kidd
Active as a pirate
1697–1699

Pirates sailed in the Indian Ocean because it offered them the chance to get rich – many merchant ships crossed the ocean to take valuable goods to the markets of Europe. The scoundrels also robbed **vessels** taking Muslim **pilgrims** to Arabia, and ships carrying cargoes to India.

In search of prey

There was one type of ship that Indian Ocean pirates preyed on more than any other.

It was a merchant ship called an **East Indiaman**. Pirates regarded these large, slow-moving vessels as their prizes. East Indiamen were cargo ships sent by countries in Europe to collect valuable goods from countries in Asia. As they sailed east towards Asia across the Indian Ocean, pirates searched for them. They knew that on board would be silver coins, and possibly gold **ingots**, which were to be traded for goods. A single ship might be carrying as much as £50,000 (about £5 million in today's money) in silver and gold.

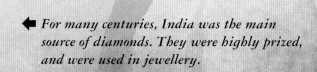

◀ *For many centuries, India was the main source of diamonds. They were highly prized, and were used in jewellery.*

The East Indiamen were most vulnerable on their way home. Heavy with cargo, they were slow-moving targets for plundering pirates. To protect themselves, these ships were armed with cannon. They often sailed in **convoys**, or groups, and sometimes they were guarded by navy warships.

◀ *East Indiamen were large, heavy ships that sat low in the water. Smaller, lighter ships were used to carry cargoes to and from them.*

▲ *Cannon balls were fired by East Indiamen. They were made from solid iron and smashed through the hull and masts of enemy ships.*

Treasures of the east

There were rich pickings for pirates who sailed in the Indian Ocean.

East Indiamen ships sailing back to Europe were loaded with cargoes of spice, tea, silk, ivory, diamonds, rubies and **porcelain**. All of these were luxury goods that only the richest people in Europe could afford to buy. Some of this **booty** could be very bulky, so pirates didn't want to hold onto it for very long. They usually sold it in local markets – as William Kidd did when he sold most of the cargo from the *Quedah Merchant* an Indian market for about £7000.

▼ *According to legend, William Kidd buried a haul of treasure somewhere in the Indian Ocean. Treasure hunters have searched for it, without success.*

◄ *Spices and tea took up a lot of room on a ship and could be difficult for pirates to sell. They often dumped these goods into the sea.*

⬆ *An East Indiaman cargo ship sinks to the bottom of the sea after being raided by pirates in the Indian Ocean.*

SHIVER ME TIMBERS!

In 1695, Henry Every raided the Indian treasure ship *Gang-i-Sawai* in the Red Sea. He got away with gold and jewels said to be worth £325,000 – billions in today's money.

It didn't take pirates of the Indian Ocean long to discover what treasures were carried on board **pilgrim ships**. Each year, a fleet of 20 or 30 ships sailed from India to Arabia, taking Muslims on the first stage of their journey to the holy city of Mecca. Indian merchants travelled with the pilgrims to Arabia, where they traded cloth and spice for gold and jewels. On their way back to India, the pilgrim ships became easy targets for European pirates.

William Kidd: the unlucky pirate

William Kidd never set out to be a pirate. For many years, he worked as a privateer in the Caribbean, where he had permission to raid French ships.

He did a good job and became quite well known. In 1695, he travelled to London and went into business with two men. They gave him a ship, the *Adventure Galley*. The plan was for Kidd to catch pirates, take their loot, then share it with his business partners. The plan didn't work.

◀ *Kidd fought with William Moore, hitting him with a bucket bound with iron hoops.*

Soon after the *Adventure Galley* entered the Indian Ocean, Kidd's **crew** tried to take control. Kidd hit one of the **mutineers**, William Moore, with a wooden bucket and killed him. Kidd continued on his journey, but instead of catching pirates he seized the *Quedah Merchant*.

Kidd thought he would be safe in America, but he wasn't. He was sent to England to stand trial for his crimes.

It was an Indian merchant ship, and by attacking without permission, Kidd had become a pirate. He kept the *Quedah Merchant* and gave her a new name – the *Adventure Prize*. Kidd sailed the *Adventure Prize* to America, where he was arrested and sent to London, England, to be tried as a pirate and a murderer. He was found guilty and sentenced to death.

William Kidd

Born: c.1645, in Scotland

Died: 1701, in London

Occupation: Privateer and pirate

The Adventure Galley:
a pirate rowing ship

In 1695, William Kidd took command of the Adventure Galley, a three-masted vessel with a crew of about 150 men.

It was designed for sailing fast, but when the wind didn't fill the sails, there was another way to move the wooden ship through the water. The ship was a **galley**, which meant it had oars. On calm days, the crew pulled on 36 oars and rowed it along. It was hard, back-breaking work, but it meant the *Adventure Galley* could close in on ships when there was no wind. Enemy ships would be going nowhere, but all the time the *Adventure Galley* would be rowing closer to them.

Mizzen mast

Gunport

Ship's lantern

➡ *Cross-section through Kidd's first ship, the* Adventure Galley, *showing its decks, guns and oars.*

Powder and shot store

SHIVER ME TIMBERS!

In 1999, a shipwreck was discovered in a bay on Madagascar. The ship had been burned, so it could be the wreck of the *Adventure Galley*.

Unfortunately for Kidd, the *Adventure Galley* was a leaky ship. He sailed it to Madagascar where he removed all the cannon, set it on fire and left it to sink. He put the cannon on his new ship, the *Adventure Prize*.

Foremast

Main mast

Bowsprit

Rowers

Drinking water casks

Oars

Adventure Galley

Built: 1695, Deptford shipyard, London

Abandoned: 1698, Madagascar

Weight: 285 tonnes

Length: 38 metres

Masts: 3

Guns: 34 cannon

73

A hard life at sea

When a man agreed to become a sea-robber, he signed the ship's articles, which was a list of rules.

The pirates who sailed with William Kidd signed articles that promised them a share of any booty taken from a prize ship. However, if they didn't obey orders, they would be punished according to the rules – **marooning** was to be left on a remote island and **keel-hauling** was to be dragged under the ship.

SHIVER ME TIMBERS!

A pirate captain dreaded the rumbling sound of a cannon ball rolling across the ship's deck. It was a signal from the crew that they were going to take control – a **mutiny** was about to happen.

← If a man didn't drown while being keel-hauled, he might die later from cuts caused as he was dragged across sharp barnacles on the ship's hull.

74

↑ *The crew on a pirate ship worked hard, under the captain's orders.*

A pirate ship could be away at sea for many months. This was always tough on the crew, as food and water would start to run out and they would have to go onto **rations**. There might be problems with the ship, as with Kidd's *Adventure Galley*, which was scrapped because of its rotten hull. Worst of all, the pirates might not find a prize, which could lead to unrest.

Articles of William Kidd

1. If a man loses an eye, leg or arm, he shall receive 600 pieces of eight, or six able slaves.
2. The man who is first to see the sail of a prize ship shall receive 100 pieces of eight.
3. Any man who disobeys a command shall lose his share and be punished as the captain deems fit.
4. Any man proved a coward in time of engagement shall lose his share.
5. Any man drunk in time of engagement shall lose his share.
6. Any man that talks of mutiny shall lose his share and be punished as the captain deems fit.
7. Any man that cheats the captain or company of any treasure, money, goods, or any other thing whatsoever to the value of one piece of eight shall lose his share and be left upon the first inhabited island the ship shall touch at.
8. Any money or treasure taken shall be shared amongst the ship's company.

Thomas Tew: the Rhode Island pirate

Thomas Tew was one of the pirates that William Kidd was supposed to catch, but never did.

Tew was based at Rhode Island, USA, and like Kidd, he started as a **privateer** before turning to piracy. Tew's ship, the *Amity*, was a **sloop**. This was a small, fast vessel that was perfect for pirates.

Thomas Tew

Born: date not known, in England

Died: 1695, in the Red Sea

Occupation: Privateer and pirate

⬆ *In 1694, Thomas Tew (left) visited Benjamin Fletcher (right), the governor of New York, USA. Tew presented Fletcher with jewels that he had plundered from ships in the Red Sea.*

76

In 1693, Tew captured a valuable Indian merchant ship in the Red Sea. He plundered its gold and gemstones, and threw the rest of the bulky cargo overboard as it was of no value to him. The haul of treasure was shared between the ship's **company**, and each man received £3000 – a huge amount of money for the time.

⬆ *The pirate flag of Thomas Tew.*

⬅ *Tew met a grisly end. He was blown apart by a cannon ball fired from the* Fateh Mohammed *as he tried to take over the ship.*

Tew joined up with Henry Every, another pirate of the Indian Ocean. They put together a small fleet of pirate ships and began to plague the Red Sea – but not for long. In 1695, during an attack on an Indian vessel, Tew was killed by a cannon ball that hit him in the stomach.

Henry Every: the successful pirate

Very few pirates got away with their crimes, except for Henry Every.

He was a master of disguise who used a false name – his real name might have been Benjamin Bridgeman, which is why one of his nicknames was 'Long Ben'.

↑ *Henry Every's success as a pirate in the Indian Ocean earned him a fortune. In the background, his ship attacks a treasure ship.*

Every began as a privateer in the Caribbean, raiding French settlements on the island of Martinique. All this changed in 1694, when he led a mutiny and took control of a ship, which he renamed the *Fancy*. He then sailed into the Indian Ocean, where he teamed up with Thomas Tew and other European pirates.

His greatest prize was the *Gang-i-Sawai*, an Indian treasure ship in the Red Sea. After a battle lasting two hours, the merchant ship surrendered, and Every helped himself to £600,000 in gold, silver and gems. After the booty was shared amongst the pirate fleet, Every sailed back to the Caribbean and disappeared.

▼ *Every led a fleet of pirate ships. They preyed on Muslim pilgrim ships returning to India with luxury goods, gold and silver.*

SHIVER ME TIMBERS!

Some of Every's crew returned to England, where they were caught and hanged. As for Every, it is thought that he settled in Ireland, where he changed his identity and lived off his ill-gotten gains.

Henry Every, known as 'Long Ben'

Born: c.1653, in England

Died: date and place not known

Occupation: Pirate

Madagascar: a pirate haven

William Kidd knew he would be safe once he reached Madagascar.

This large island, off the east coast of Africa, was a haven for pirates, and it was where Kidd abandoned the leaky *Adventure Galley* in 1698. Madagascar was on a busy **trade route**, and East Indiamen sailing to and from Europe and North America sailed close by. Each passing merchant ship was a potential prize for a plundering pirate.

Pirate colonies grew up on the east side of Madagascar, and by 1720 there were about 1500 pirates there. Many had fled to Madagascar from the Caribbean, after the authorities there had clamped down on them. Traders worked in the colonies, selling everyday goods to pirates in exchange for their stolen booty.

⬆ *On Madagascar, European traders sold guns, swords, gunpowder and alcohol to the island's pirates.*

▲ *Squadrons of British battleships were sent to Madagascar – the pirates were no match for these heavily-armed ships with men trained for war.*

The pirates became such a nuisance that something had to be done to protect shipping. In the 1720s, warships of the British Royal Navy began cruising near Madagascar, and the pirate menace faded away.

SHIVER ME TIMBERS!

Life was hard for pirates on Madagascar. They were often killed by disease, or in fights with local people or pirate gangs.

The Angrias: a family of pirates

Pirates from Europe were not the only menace in the Indian Ocean – there were also plenty of local pirates.

The most notorious was the Angria family, who plundered ships of all nations. Piracy was their way of life, passed on from father to son. The Angrias were masters of the west coast of India for about 50 years, from 1700 to 1750. They stopped ships that crossed into their territory and forced the captains to give them money. In return, the Angrias let the ships carry on their journeys – but not always.

➤ *Shackles were locked around a prisoner's ankles or wrists.*

SHIVER ME TIMBERS!

Conajee Angria kept an English merchant, Peter Curgenven, captive for about five years. He had to wear chains called **shackles**, which injured his legs. When Curgenven was released, a doctor cut off his worst leg and Curgenven bled to death.

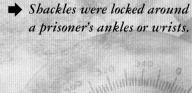

In 1704, the British told Conajee Angria to leave their ships alone. He refused. In 1707, he attacked the *Bombay*, a British East Indiaman, and he went on to raid many others. In 1736, Conajee's son, Sumbhajee, plundered the *Derby* and a fortune in gold was seized. The end came in 1756, when a fleet of British warships destroyed 65 Angria pirate ships and took their treasure.

⬆ *The Angria fleet (the smaller ships) attacked British merchant ships off the coast of India in 1740.*

Conajee Angria

Born: date not known, in India

Died: 1729, in India

Occupation: Pirate

⬅ *Conajee Angria was the leader of a family of Indian pirates.*

Edward England:
the kind-hearted pirate

Edward England became a pirate in 1717, when pirates took over the ship he was on – he decided to join them.

At first, England worked as a pirate in the Caribbean, until he was forced to flee in 1718. He sailed to Africa, where he plundered ships along the west coast and in the Indian Ocean.

➤ *In one raid, England used a fireship (a burning ship) against two vessels he hoped to capture. The plan failed, and the ships escaped.*

England gave one of his prize ships to one of his crew, John Taylor. In 1720, England attacked the *Cassandra*, a British East Indiaman. In the battle, off the coast of Madagascar, 90 of England's pirate crew were killed, but they managed to seize the *Cassandra*.

Edward England

Born: date not known, in Ireland

Died: c.1721, on Madagascar

Occupation: Pirate

England took the cargo, said to be worth £75,000. He let the crew go free, which made John Taylor very angry. He said that England should have killed the crew in revenge for the loss of so many of their pirate comrades. The men agreed with Taylor, and they made him their captain, in place of England.

➡ *The pirate flag of Edward England.*

Sentenced to death

Most pirates came to miserable ends.

Thomas Tew was killed by a cannon ball, Edward England spent his last days as a beggar, and William Kidd was hanged – not once, but twice. If a pirate was caught by the authorities, he was almost certain to be sentenced to death, and that meant being hanged by the neck until dead.

⬇ *The trial of William Kidd was held in London, England, in 1701.*

In 1699, William Kidd was arrested in Boston, USA, and was sent to trial in England. At this time, parts of North America were controlled by England, which is why his trial was held there. In May 1701, Kidd was found guilty of murdering William Moore, the sailor he hit with a bucket, and of robbing the *Quedah Merchant*.

Kidd was sentenced to hang. On the first attempt, the hangman's rope snapped, and Kidd fell to the ground, very much alive. He was led back up to the **scaffold**, and a new noose was put around his neck. This one didn't break.

⬇ *Kidd's dead body was hanged in chains – an iron cage that kept his remains together while they slowly rotted away.*

SHIVER ME TIMBERS!

Kidd's body was placed inside an iron cage and left to hang on the shore of the River Thames at Tilbury, near London. Birds pecked at the body and it slowly rotted. It was a grisly sight, meant to stop other men from becoming pirates.

87

Blackbeard

and the
Pirates of the Caribbean

CONTENTS

Pirate attack!

In November 1717, a pirate ship sailed off the coast of Martinique Island, in the Caribbean Sea.

Its captain was Edward Teach, known as Blackbeard. His ship was a **sloop** – a small, fast **vessel** with a single **mast**, 12 **cannon** and a **crew** of about 120 pirates.

A larger ship came into view, and Blackbeard set a course towards it. It was the *Concorde*, a French **merchant ship**. It was packed with more than 400 slaves from Africa. The *Concorde* was well armed, but after four months crossing the Atlantic Ocean, the crew was in no mood for a fight. Blackbeard fired his cannon as a warning, and the captain of the *Concorde* surrendered his ship without a struggle.

⬆ The Concorde *was bigger and better armed than Blackbeard's sloop – but Blackbeard was determined to seize it.*

SHIVER ME TIMBERS!

The *Concorde* was carrying treasure – about 9 kilograms of gold dust, plus silver and jewellery. The ship's cabin boy, 15-year-old Louis Arot, told Blackbeard where it was hidden. Instead of sailing away with the rest of the *Concorde*'s crew, Arot became one of Blackbeard's pirates.

The pirates put the *Concorde*'s crew and slaves onto Blackbeard's sloop, and let them sail away. The *Concorde* was the **prize**, and it became Blackbeard's **flagship**. It came with about 16 cannon, but Blackbeard increased the number to 40, and he gave the ship a new name – the *Queen Anne's Revenge*.

Pirates of the Caribbean: 1690–1730

Blackbeard was one of many pirates who terrorized the Caribbean.

For about 40 years, from 1690 to 1730, sea-robbers raided towns and **plundered** ships that crossed their path. This was the Golden Age of Caribbean piracy.

Before the Caribbean became the haunt of pirates, it was home to **buccaneers**. They were mainly English, French and Dutch men who lived on the Caribbean's many islands. In the 1600s, some island **governors** gave the buccaneers permission to raid Spanish ships, which they did with great success. When buccaneers began plundering ships from *every* country, the governors tried to put an end to their activities – without success.

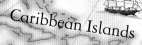

⬆ *Caribbean pirates cruised the waters around the sea's many islands, from the north-east coast of South America to the east coast of the United States.*

Some buccaneers carried on raiding without permission – and that is when they became pirates. Hundreds of men and a few women sailed as pirates in the Caribbean. Like Blackbeard, they were attracted by thoughts of rich pickings. For a few years, they were masters of the Caribbean.

North America

Caribbean Islands

Caribbean Sea

South America

ROGUES' GALLERY

Henry Morgan
Active as a buccaneer
1665–1671

Samuel Bellamy
Active as a pirate
1715–1717

Edward Teach
Active as a pirate
1716–1718

John Rackham
Active as a pirate
1718–1720

Anne Bonny
Active as a pirate
1719–1720

Mary Read
Active as a pirate
1719–1720

93

Pirate ship: a den of thieves

Most pirate ships in the Caribbean were sloops. Pirates used sloops because they were faster than the merchant ships they raided.

Once a pirate sloop set course towards a merchant ship, it soon caught up with the bigger, slower vessel, as Blackbeard did when he attacked the *Concorde*. A fast ship also meant that pirates could escape to safety when navy warships came after them.

➡ *A typical 12-gun sloop used by Caribbean pirates. It was about 18 metres in length and weighed about 100 tonnes.*

Windlass

The best sloops were built in the shipyards of Jamaica and Bermuda. They had single masts and could sail in shallow water. They could come close to land without getting stuck, and hide in sheltered bays. Pirate captains fitted their sloops with many cannon, which they took from captured ships.

Anchor

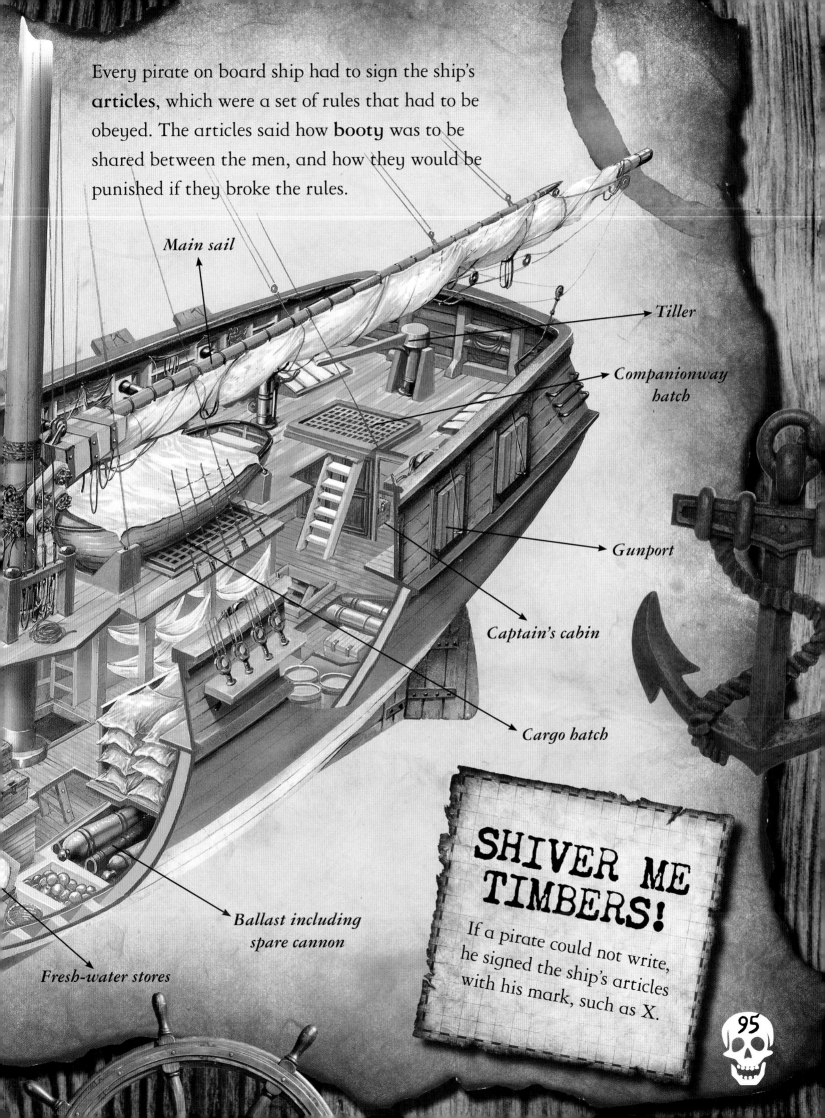

Every pirate on board ship had to sign the ship's **articles**, which were a set of rules that had to be obeyed. The articles said how **booty** was to be shared between the men, and how they would be punished if they broke the rules.

Main sail

Tiller

Companionway hatch

Gunport

Captain's cabin

Cargo hatch

Ballast including spare cannon

Fresh-water stores

SHIVER ME TIMBERS!

If a pirate could not write, he signed the ship's articles with his mark, such as X.

Sir Henry Morgan: the king's favourite

Henry Morgan was a buccaneer. At the end of 1667, the governor of Jamaica, Thomas Modyford, gave him permission to attack Spanish ships, since he believed Spain was planning to invade the island.

Morgan had other plans. In January 1668, he raided a Spanish town on Cuba and then, with a force of 500 men, captured Portobello, a Spanish port on the coast of Panama. He returned to Jamaica with a fortune said to be worth £100,000.

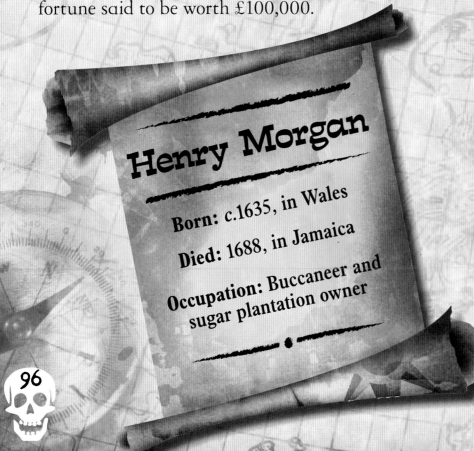

Henry Morgan

Born: c.1635, in Wales

Died: 1688, in Jamaica

Occupation: Buccaneer and sugar plantation owner

⬆ *In 1669, Morgan attacked and burned Spanish ships off the coast of Venezuela, and took 20,000 silver pesos from them.*

In 1670, Governor Modyford sent Morgan back to Panama, this time with 2000 men. Unfortunately for Morgan, the Spaniards had moved their treasure out of the city, leaving little to steal. Worse was to come – Spain and England had signed a **peace treaty**. When Morgan returned to Jamaica, he was arrested and sent to England.

⬆ *Morgan forced the citizens of Portobello to hand over 100,000 silver pesos. Only after the ransom had been paid, did Morgan leave their town.*

Morgan spent two years in the Tower of London, but was never charged with any crime. In fact, he became a hero for his actions against Spain, England's old enemy. On his release, Morgan was **knighted** by King Charles II, and in 1675, he returned to Jamaica as the island's lieutenant-governor.

Edward Teach: the most notorious pirate

Edward Teach, better known as Blackbeard, was a tall man with wild eyes.

His long, black beard was twisted with ribbons, lengths of smoking **fuse** poked out from under his hat, and across his chest were slings that held six pistols. Blackbeard looked tough, and he was tough.

⬆ A *flintlock pistol* fired a small ball of solid lead, and took a long time to reload. In close combat, the handle was used as a club.

Blackbeard's reign of terror began in 1716, when he joined the pirate Benjamin Hornigold. Blackbeard was soon in command of a sloop, which he replaced with a larger ship, the *Queen Anne's Revenge*. As Blackbeard plundered ships and towns along the east coast of North America, he earned a reputation as a fierce pirate. He was so ruthless that he even **marooned** his own men, and made off with all the booty.

Blackbeard met his end in November 1718, when he was tracked down by Lieutenant Robert Maynard of the British Royal Navy. He was killed by a sword blow from one of Maynard's men, and his head was cut off and put on the **bow** of Maynard's ship for all to see.

Edward Teach
known as 'Blackbeard'

Born: c.1680, in England

Died: 1718, off the coast of North Carolina, North America

Occupation: Pirate

◀ *Blackbeard's last moments, as he fights to the death with Lieutenant Maynard on board the Royal Navy ship the* Jane.

SHIVER ME TIMBERS!

A shipwreck, believed to be the *Queen Anne's Revenge*, was found in 1996. Archaeologists are studying the wreck to see if it really could be Blackbeard's famous ship.

99

Life on board ship

Pirate sloops sailed with a **company**, or crew, of about 80 men.

The crew was very well organized and discipline was important. As well as agreeing to keep the ship's articles, each pirate knew his place in the company. The captain was in charge, helped by the **quartermaster**, who was second-in-command.

◄ *Wooden barrels stored the crew's food and other supplies. Each one was made from pieces of strong wood, held together with iron hoops.*

There was always boring, everyday work for the men to do. Swords were kept sharp, cannon were cleaned and made ready for use, torn sails were mended, meals were prepared and lookouts kept watch for ships and land.

◄ *Sails were made from coarse cloth called canvas. Rips had to be stitched up.*

What the men wanted most of all was a chance to raise the ship's flag, or **Jolly Roger**, which was a sign that they were pirates. Pirate captains had their own flags, showing skulls, bones, swords and wounded hearts, usually on a black background. These designs signalled 'death' to anyone who resisted.

SHIVER ME TIMBERS!

Live sea turtles were kept on board some pirate ships. They were a source of fresh meat for Caribbean pirates.

100

PIRATE FLAGS

The name 'Jolly Roger' might come from the French words jolie rouge meaning 'pretty red', or from the English word 'roger' meaning 'devil'.

Edward Teach, known as Blackbeard

Bartholomew Roberts

John Rackham

Stede Bonnet

Pirate havens

Dotted around the Caribbean were safe havens where pirates anchored their ships and came ashore.

The buccaneers used Port Royal, on the island of Jamaica, as their den. In its **taverns**, they gambled and drank away the proceeds of their raids until, in 1692, the town was destroyed by an earthquake.

⬆ *Port Royal was destroyed by an earthquake, and much of the town was swallowed by the sea.*

In the Golden Age of piracy — the time of Blackbeard, Samuel Bellamy, John Rackham and others — the island of New Providence became the Caribbean's major pirate haven.

Speak like a pirate

Ahoy! Shouted to a ship or a person to attract attention.

Avast! A command, meaning to stop doing something.

Davy Jones' Locker The bottom of the sea — home of shipwrecks and drowned sailors.

Land ho! Shouted by the ship's lookout when land was sighted.

Lubber A clumsy person not used to life at sea.

Mate A fellow sailor. Also an officer on a merchant or navy ship.

Swabber The lowest type of sailor, only fit for swabbing (mopping) the decks.

Their sloops took shelter in the island's shallow harbour, where the bigger pirate-hunting warships of the British Royal Navy could not enter. The island provided pirates with food, water and timber. Bribes were given to the island's governors, and in return, the pirates were left alone.

By 1717, about 500 pirates used New Providence as their base. However, when Governor Woodes Rogers came to the island the following year, he hanged eight of them and **pardoned** those who gave up piracy. Some, including Blackbeard, fled to new havens.

SHIVER ME TIMBERS!

After leaving New Providence, Blackbeard made Ocracoke Island his base, from where he raided towns along the east coast of North America.

↓ *Woodes Rogers was originally a privateer. He had permission from the English government to raid Spanish ships and settlements.*

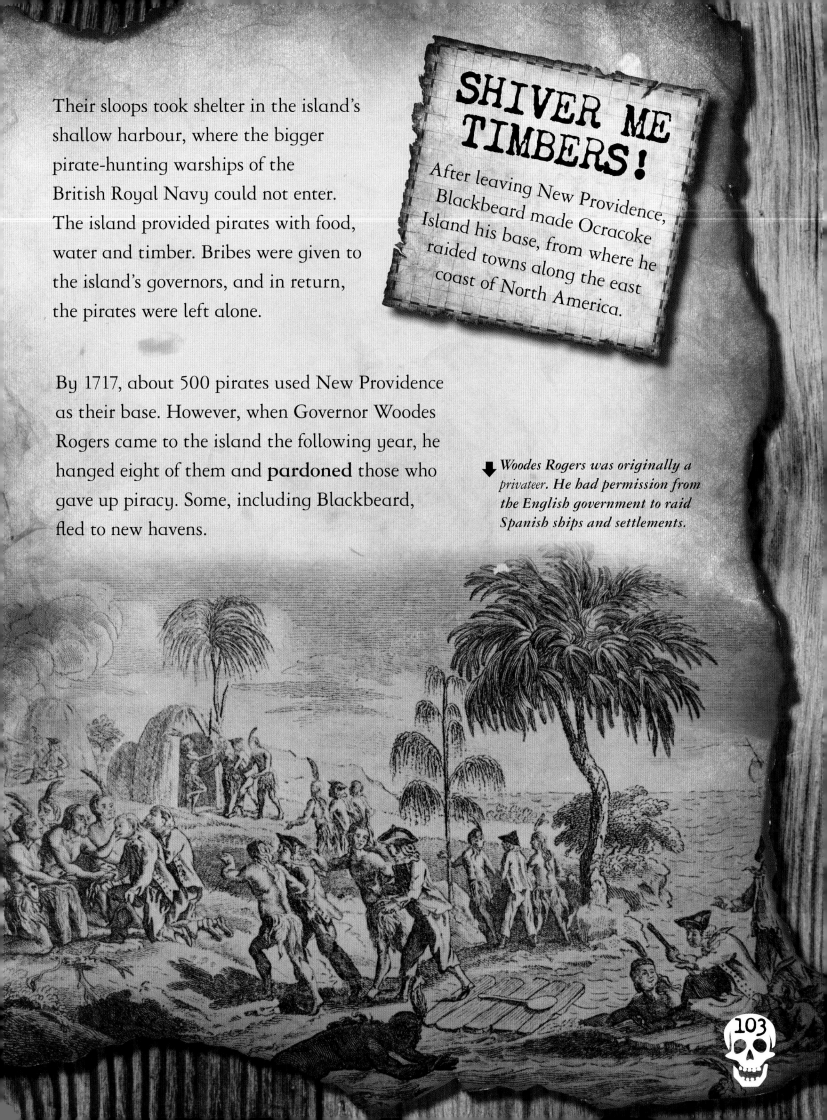

Samuel Bellamy: the pirate prince

Samuel Bellamy was known as the prince of pirates by his men because he gave them equal shares in any loot he took.

In March 1717, Bellamy sailed from the pirate haven of New Providence in his sloop the *Sultana*. He was in search of a prize and it was not long before he spotted a large merchant ship. It was the *Whydah*, a slave ship. It had delivered its human cargo to Jamaica and was now bound for England, loaded with ivory, indigo, sugar and thousands of Spanish gold and silver coins.

SHIVER ME TIMBERS!

The wreck of the *Whydah* was found by a treasure hunter in 1984. It was the first pirate ship found in the Caribbean, and some of its valuable treasure has been salvaged.

↑ The Whydah *ran aground, broke apart and sank. Bellamy and 143 other pirates were drowned. Only two men survived.*

104

A Spanish gold coin and ring from the wreck of the Whydah. Thousands of coins, gold bars and pieces of jewellery have been brought to the surface.

Samuel Bellamy

Born: 1689, in England

Died: 1717, off the coast of Massachusetts, North America

Occupation: Pirate

Bellamy chased the *Whydah* for three days, and captured it near the Bahamas. The ship was one of the most valuable prizes ever taken by a Caribbean pirate, and Bellamy made it his flagship. However, his luck soon ran out. In May 1717, the *Whydah* was wrecked in a storm. Bellamy and most of his crew were drowned, and the pirate treasure disappeared into Davy Jones' Locker – the bottom of the sea.

Pirate prizes: ships and their cargoes

On a clear day, a pirate lookout could see a ship up to 32 kilometres away.

It was important to identify the ship quickly. Pirate sloops kept well away from warships, which could be on anti-piracy patrol. What the pirates wanted was a merchant ship, and when one was sighted, they sailed towards it. As their sloop caught up with the prize, the pirates flew a false flag.

➡ *From high in the ship's rigging, a lookout kept watch for ships to raid as well as ships to avoid.*

This tricked the captain of the merchant ship into thinking that the sloop was friendly, so he did not try to escape. When the pirates were close, they raised their pirate flag and fired their cannon over the bow of the prize, hoping the captain would surrender without a fight.

➡ *Caribbean pirates fought with cutlass swords. They were slashing weapons and were sharp along one edge.*

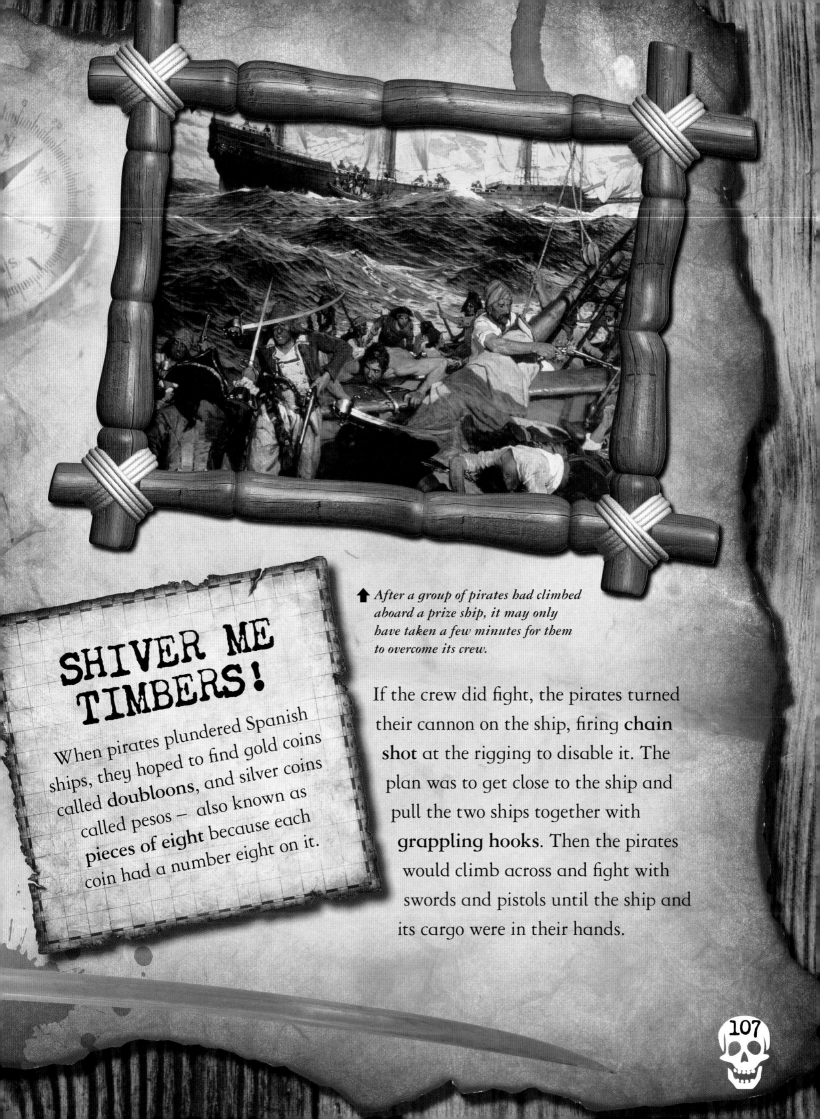

↑ *After a group of pirates had climbed aboard a prize ship, it may only have taken a few minutes for them to overcome its crew.*

SHIVER ME TIMBERS!

When pirates plundered Spanish ships, they hoped to find gold coins called **doubloons**, and silver coins called pesos — also known as **pieces of eight** because each coin had a number eight on it.

If the crew did fight, the pirates turned their cannon on the ship, firing **chain shot** at the rigging to disable it. The plan was to get close to the ship and pull the two ships together with **grappling hooks**. Then the pirates would climb across and fight with swords and pistols until the ship and its cargo were in their hands.

John Rackham:
the pirate in fancy clothes

John, or Jack, Rackham wore striped shirts made from **calico**, which earned him the nickname 'Calico Jack'.

Rackham was one of the many pirates who used the island of New Providence as a base. When Woodes Rogers became the governor there in 1718, Rackham accepted his pardon and agreed to give up piracy. It did not last long. There was little work on the island, so Rackham went back to being a pirate.

⬆ *This early picture of John Rackham shows him as a tall, well-dressed man. He is carrying a sword and a pistol.*

John Rackham

Born: not known

Died: 1720, in Jamaica

Occupation: Pirate

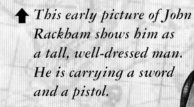

John Rackham and his men were executed in 1720.

Rackham gathered a small crew, including women – Anne Bonny and Mary Read. They sailed on the sloop the *William*, and for a year they plundered small ships, but the booty did not amount to much.

A boarding axe used by pirates. It was also good for slicing through ropes.

Governor Rogers sent pirate hunter Captain Jonathan Barnet to catch Rackham. After a brief skirmish, Rackham and his crew were rounded up. Rackham and ten male pirates were hanged at Port Royal, Jamaica. His body was left hanging at the entrance to the harbour as a grim warning to others.

Anne Bonny and Mary Read

Anne Bonny and Mary Read were brought up as boys.

Bonny married a penniless sailor, and they made their way to the island of New Providence, where she met the pirate John Rackham. Read became a soldier, and fought in northern Europe. Then she sailed to the Caribbean, where she also met Rackham. He persuaded the women to join his company and their lives changed forever.

Anne Bonny

Born: 1698, in Ireland

Died: 1782, in South Carolina, North America

Occupation: Pirate

▼ *Anne Bonny and Mary Read disguised themselves as men.*

Rackham's arrest caused a sensation. When Captain Jonathan Barnet caught up with him, Rackham and most of his crew were too drunk to fight. Only two of the company fought back. When they were overpowered, they were found to be women dressed as men – Bonny and Read. The women were sentenced to hang, along with Rackham and his men. However, as both of them were pregnant, they were allowed to live.

↑ *The courtroom at St Jago de la Vega, Jamaica, where Rackham, Bonny, Read and the other members of Rackham's crew were sent for trial.*

Mary Read

Born: c.1695, in England

Died: 1721, in Jamaica

Occupation: Pirate

Punishments for prisoners and pirates

When pirates captured a ship or raided a town, they sometimes took prisoners.

Prisoners were usually held in return for goods or valuable information. Blackbeard once traded a group of prisoners for a chest of medicine – an odd trade for a pirate to make! If pirates thought that their prisoners knew where treasure was, they had ways of getting the information out of them, all of which involved cruelty.

▶ *The cat o' nine tails was a leather whip with several strands. Along the strands were sharp pieces of metal and pins.*

It was the quartermaster's job to make prisoners speak up, which many did before they were punished. The very thought of being **flogged** with the **cat o' nine tails** was often enough to loosen a prisoner's tongue.

◀ *Towing was a punishment used to weaken a man. If he failed to keep his head above the water, he drowned.*

112

Marooning meant that a man was left alone on an island. He could wait for years before another ship came his way.

The quartermaster carried out some of the worst punishments on pirates themselves. It was a way of keeping the company disciplined, letting the crew know what would happen if they disobeyed orders or broke the ship's articles. Pirates of the Caribbean never made a person 'walk the plank' – a made-up punishment used in storybooks and films.

Pirate punishments

Blooding Pricked and spiked with knives and pins.

Ducking Splashed up and down in the sea.

Flogging Lashed with the cat o' nine tails.

Hanging Hanged by the neck until dead.

Keel-hauling Dragged under the ship, side to side.

Man overboard Thrown off the ship, and left to drown.

Marooning Abandoned on an island.

Moses' law Given 39 lashes with the cat.

One man island Left to drift with a plank of wood.

Towing Pulled along at the end of a rope behind the ship.

Pirate hunters: the end of pirates in the Caribbean

Pirates were masters of the Caribbean for only a few years and most had very short careers.

The end began when places such as New Providence stopped being safe havens for them. When Woodes Rogers became governor there, the first thing he did was offer a pardon to about 500 pirates.

SHIVER ME TIMBERS!

The bodies of some executed pirates, like John Rackham's, were wrapped in chains or iron cages and left to hang, where they slowly rotted away. It was a grisly sight, and was meant to scare people off becoming pirates themselves.

Many accepted it, and in return for giving up piracy they were left alone. However, some pirates could not, or would not, change their 'vile course of life', as Governor Rogers described piracy. These were the pirates who were tracked down by pirate hunters, sent out by governors to bring them to justice.

← *Despite having many cannon on their ships, pirates were outgunned by the pirate hunters who came after them.*

▲ Bartholmew Roberts was killed by grapeshot fired from a navy warship (left). His men threw his body into the sea, rather than letting the naval officers hang it in chains.

Pirates were rounded up and executed, often in groups. In 1718, Stede Bonnet was hanged with 30 others in Charleston, North Carolina. In 1722, 40 pirates were sent to the **gallows** in Kingston, Jamaica, and the following year, 26 men came to the same end in Newport, Rhode Island. By 1730, the pirates of the Caribbean had been defeated.

◄ Stede Bonnet was hanged for piracy in 1718. He held onto a small bunch of flowers – a sign that he was sorry for all the wrong that he had done.

GLOSSARY

Ancestor A past member of someone's family.

Archaeologist A person who studies the remains of the past, on land and under water.

Articles A set of rules that pirates were expected to follow.

Bagnio A type of prison in north Africa where slaves were held prisoner.

Barbary Coast An area of the north African coast, from modern-day Algeria to Libya, which was home to corsairs.

Blockade To seal off a place, stopping people and goods from going in and out.

Booty Goods stolen by thieves. Also called loot or plunder.

Bow The front of a ship.

Buccaneer An outlaw who lived on the Caribbean islands and became a pirate.

Calico A type of fine cotton fabric.

Cannon A large gun or guns on wheels that fired cannon balls and other types of shot.

Cargo The goods carried on a ship.

Castle On a sailing ship, the raised platform at the bow, or front, and stern, or back.

Cat o' nine tails A whip of nine knotted rope cords fastened to a handle. It was used against crew members and prisoners.

Chain shot A type of shot fired from a cannon – two iron balls joined by a chain.

Christian Someone who believes in the ideas taught by Jesus Christ.

Circumnavigate To travel all the way round the world.

City-state A self-governing city and its land.

Colony A country or area under the control of a more powerful country.

Company The crew of a pirate ship.

Convoy A group of ships travelling together.

Corsair A pirate or privateer who operated in the Mediterranean Sea.

Crew The people who worked on a ship. Also called the company.

Cutlass A short sword with a slightly curved blade.

Doubloon A Spanish gold coin used in Spain and the Caribbean.

Dysentery A disease that causes severe sickness, leading to weight loss, dehydration and death.

East Indiaman A large, slow-moving sailing ship used to transport goods. A merchant ship.

Escort ship A ship that protects other ships from attack.

Flagship The main ship used by a pirate captain or navy commander.

Fleet A group of ships sailing together.

Flintlock pistol A type of pistol fired by a spark from a piece of flint.

Flog To lash, or beat, with a whip or stick.

Forecastle The raised platform at the bow, or front, of a sailing ship.

Fuse A piece of material that a flame travels along to ignite, or set off, an explosion.

Galiot A small galley ship.

Galleon A large, slow-moving sailing ship used to transport goods.

Galley A type of ship powered through the water by oars.

Gallows A structure used for killing criminals by hanging them from a rope.

Governor A person in charge of a place.

Grapeshot A type of shot fired from a cannon – a mass of small iron balls.

Grappling hook A four-pronged iron hook on a rope. It was used to pull one ship alongside another ship, so it could be boarded.

Gruel Boiled cereal, like porridge.

Gunpowder A fine, black powder that burns easily. It was used to fire handguns and cannon.

Halberd An axe at the end of a long pole.

Haven A safe place, or a hideaway.

Holy war A war fought between sides that have different religious beliefs.

Ingot A block of metal, such as gold or silver.

Islam The Muslim religion. The holy book is the Koran.

Jerkin A jacket made from padded leather.

Jolly Roger The nickname for any pirate flag.

Keel-haul To be hauled or dragged under a ship from one side to the other.

Knight To give someone the title of knight as a reward.

Letter of Marque A licence given to a privateer by his government or ruler, giving him permission to raid enemy towns and ships.

Loot Goods stolen by thieves. Also called booty or plunder.

Maroon To abandon, or leave, on an island.

Mast A tall pole that the sails of a ship hang on.

Merchant ship A ship designed to transport goods.

Mizzen mast On a sailing ship, the mast at the stern, or back.

Moor To secure a ship to the shore by means of a rope or cable.

Musket A hand gun with a long barrel.

Muslim Someone who follows the religion of Islam.

Mutineer A person who refuses to take orders from a ship's captain.

Mutiny When the crew take control of a ship from its captain.

Papal Relating to the Pope.

Pardon To forgive mistakes or offences, or to cancel a person's punishment.

Peace treaty When opposite sides agree to be on friendly, peaceful terms.

Peso A Spanish silver coin used in Spain and the Caribbean. Also known as a piece of eight because it had the number eight on it, showing it was worth eight reales.

Piece of eight The nickname for a Spanish peso or eight reales coin.

Pike A long pole with a pointed tip. A half-pike was a shorter version.

Pilgrim ship A ship taking pilgrims to a holy place.

Pilgrim A person making a journey to a holy place.

Plunder To steal, or goods stolen by thieves. Also called loot or booty.

Porcelain A type of fine, white pottery originally made in China.

Privateer A person who has permission from his government or ruler to attack and steal goods from his country's enemy.

Prize A ship taken as a reward.

Protection money Money given to someone in order to be protected against attack.

Quartermaster The second-in-command on a ship, in charge of punishments.

Ransom Money that is paid to free someone who is held as a prisoner.

Rapier A slender, sharply pointed sword, used mainly for thrusting attacks.

Rations A fixed amount of food, usually served each day.

Reis An Arabic word meaning captain or commander.

Rigging The ropes, posts and chains that hold up a ship's sails.

Sail A large piece of strong cloth on the mast of a ship, so the wind will push the boat along.

Scaffold A raised structure that was used to hang criminals them.

Shackles A pair of metal rings joined by a chain that are used to hold together a prisoner's hands or feet.

Slave A prisoner forced to do the work of their master.

Sloop A small, fast vessel.

Spanish Main Spain's empire in the Caribbean and the American mainland. At first it only referred to the northern coast of South America, but eventually it came to mean the whole of the Caribbean region.

Sterncastle The raised platform at the stern, or back, of a sailing ship.

Sultan The ruler of a Muslim country or city-state.

Swivel gun A small cannon mounted on the edge rail of a ship, which could be turned from side to side.

Tavern A place where alcoholic drinks were consumed. Another word for an inn.

Trade route A way across sea or land that was used by traders.

Treasure ship A ship used to carry treasure.

Turban A man's headdress, made by wrapping a strip of cloth around the head.

Vessel A ship or large boat.

INDEX